To: _____

From: _____

Scripture taken from the Holy Bible, King James Version.

January 1

Thou crownest the year with Thy goodness.

PSALM 65:11 KJV

December 31

*Surely goodness and mercy shall follow me all the days of my life:
and I will dwell in the house of the Lord for ever.*

PSALM 23:6 KJV

January 2

I am the Light of the world: he that followeth Me
shall not walk in darkness, but shall have the light of life.

JOHN 8:12 KJV

December 30

Peace I leave with you, My peace I give unto you.

JOHN 14:27 KJV

The Lord is my light and my salvation…
the Lord is the strength of my life.

PSALM 27:1 KJV

December 29

Blessed be His glorious name for ever:
and let the whole earth be filled with His glory.

PSALM 72:19 KJV

January 4

"*I am Alpha and Omega, the beginning and the ending,*" saith the Lord, "*which is, and which was, and which is to come, the Almighty.*"

REVELATION 1:8 KJV

December 28

Blessed be the God and Father of our Lord Jesus Christ,
which according to His abundant mercy hath begotten us again
unto a lively hope by the resurrection of Jesus Christ.

I PETER 1:3 KJV

January 5

From the rising of the sun unto the going down of the same the Lord's name is to be praised.

PSALM 113:3 KJV

December 27

Looking for that blessed hope, and the glorious appearing of the great God and our Saviour Jesus Christ.

TITUS 2:13 KJV

January 6

Now the God of hope fill you with all joy and peace in believing,
that ye may abound in hope, through the power of the Holy Ghost.

ROMANS 15:13 KJV

December 26

Mine eyes have seen Thy salvation,
which Thou hast prepared before the face of all people.

LUKE 2:30, 31 KJV

January 7

How precious also are Thy thoughts unto me, O God!
how great is the sum of them!

PSALM 139:17 KJV

December 25

Thou...shalt call His name Jesus.
He shall be great, and shall be called the Son of the Highest.

LUKE 1:31, 32 KJV

I am persuaded, that neither death, nor life…shall be able to separate us from the love of God, which is in Christ Jesus our Lord.

ROMANS 8:38, 39 KJV

December 24

Glory to God in the highest.

LUKE 2:14 KJV

January 9

He is God, the faithful God, which keepeth covenant and mercy with them that love Him and keep His commandments to a thousand generations.

DEUTERONOMY 7:8, 9 KJV

December 23

*Suddenly there was with the angel
a multitude of the heavenly host praising God.*

LUKE 2:13 KJV

January 10

Thanks be unto God,
which always causeth us to triumph in Christ.

II CORINTHIANS 2:14 KJV

December 22

Ye shall find the Babe wrapped in swaddling clothes,
lying in a manger.

LUKE 2:12 KJV

January 11

The Lord will bless His people with peace.

PSALM 29:11 KJV

December 21

*Unto you is born this day in the city of David a Saviour,
which is Christ the Lord.*

LUKE 2:11 KJV

January 12

In My Father's house are many mansions...
I go to prepare a place for you.

JOHN 14:2 KJV

December 20

*I bring you good tidings of great joy,
which shall be to all people.*

LUKE 2:10 KJV

January 13

The Lord bless thee, and keep thee: The Lord
make His face shine upon thee, and be gracious unto thee.

NUMBERS 6:24-25 KJV

December 19

The Word was made flesh, and dwelt among us.

JOHN 1:14 KJV

January 14

*Your Father knoweth what things
ye have need of, before ye ask Him.*

MATTHEW 6:8 KJV

December 18

*When the fulness of the time
was come, God sent forth His Son.*

GALATIANS 4:4 KJV

January 15

I will bless thee...and thou shalt be a blessing.

GENESIS 12:2 KJV

December 17

*God sent His only begotten Son into the world,
that we might live through Him.*

I JOHN 4:9 KJV

January 16

Well done, thou good and faithful servant.

MATTHEW 25:21 KJV

December 16

And she shall bring forth a Son, and thou shalt call His name Jesus: for He shall save His people from their sins.

MATTHEW 1:21 KJV

They that wait upon the Lord shall renew their strength;
they shall mount up with wings as eagles.

ISAIAH 40:31 KJV

December 15

Of the increase of His government and peace there shall be no end,
upon the throne of David, and upon His kingdom.

ISAIAH 9:7 KJV

January 18

*Blessed are they which do hunger and
thirst after righteousness: for they shall be filled.*

MATTHEW 5:6 KJV

December 14

Thomas Kinkade

Behold the Lamb of God,
which taketh away the sin of the world.

JOHN 1:29 KJV

January 19

The joy of the Lord is your strength.

NEHEMIAH 8:10 KJV

December 13

*Many, O Lord my God,
are Thy wonderful works which Thou hast done.*

PSALM 40:5 KJV

January 20

We have this treasure in earthen vessels, that the excellency of the power may be of God, and not of us.

II CORINTHIANS 4:7 KJV

December 12

*All that is in the heaven and in the earth is Thine; Thine is
the kingdom, O LORD, and Thou art exalted as head above all.*

I CHRONICLES 29:11 KJV

January 21

A friend loveth at all times.

PROVERBS 17:17 KJV

December 11

This is our God; we have waited for Him,
and He will save us: this is the Lord; we have waited for Him,
we will be glad and rejoice in His salvation.

ISAIAH 25:9 KJV

January 22

For He hath said, "I will never leave thee, nor forsake thee."

HEBREWS 13:5 KJV

December 10

For the Son of man is come
to seek and to save that which was lost.

LUKE 19:10 KJV

January 23

O satisfy us early with Thy mercy;
that we may rejoice and be glad all our days.

PSALM 90:14 KJV

December 9

Every good gift and every perfect gift is from above,
and cometh down from the Father of lights.

JAMES 1:17 KJV

January 24

He careth for you.

I PETER 5:7 KJV

December 8

*His name shall be called Wonderful, Counsellor,
The Mighty God, The Everlasting Father, The Prince of Peace.*

ISAIAH 9:6 KJV

January 25

He hath made every thing beautiful in His time.

ECCLESIASTES 3:11 KJV

Thanks be unto God for His unspeakable gift.

II CORINTHIANS 9:15 KJV

January 26

The times of refreshing
shall come from the presence of the Lord.

ACTS 3:19 KJV

December 6

Unto us a Child is born, unto us a Son is given.

ISAIAH 9:6 KJV

January 27

God is my strength and power: and He maketh my way perfect.

II SAMUEL 22:33 KJV

December 5

The Dayspring from on high hath visited us,
to give light to them that sit in darkness.

LUKE 1:78, 79 KJV

The God of love and peace shall be with you.

II CORINTHIANS 13:11 KJV

December 4

His mercy is on them that
fear Him from generation to generation.

LUKE 1:50 KJV

January 29

Bless the Lord, O my soul, and forget not all His benefits.

PSALM 103:2 KJV

December 3

Mary said, "My soul doth magnify the Lord,
and my spirit hath rejoiced in God my Saviour."

LUKE 1:46, 47 KJV

January 30

In Him we live, and move, and have our being.

ACTS 17:28 KJV

He shall reign over the house of Jacob for ever;
and of His kingdom there shall be no end.

LUKE 1:33 KJV

January 31

In quietness and in confidence shall be your strength.

ISAIAH 30:15 KJV

December 1

He shall be great, and shall be called the Son of the Highest:
and the Lord God shall give unto Him the throne of His father David.

LUKE 1:32 KJV

February 1

*I am come that they might have life,
and that they might have it more abundantly.*

JOHN 10:10 KJV

November 30

Truly God is good.

PSALM 73:1 KJV

February 2

Be glad and rejoice: for the Lord will do great things.

JOEL 2:21 KJV

November 29

It is a good thing to give thanks unto the Lord,
and to sing praises unto Thy name, O most High.

PSALM 92:1 KJV

February 3

God is able to make all grace abound toward you.

II CORINTHIANS 9:8 KJV

November 28

*Now therefore, our God,
we thank Thee, and praise Thy glorious name.*

I CHRONICLES 29:13 KJV

February 4

Ye shall go out with joy, and be led forth with peace.

ISAIAH 55:12 KJV

November 27

Praise ye the Lord.
O give thanks unto the Lord; for He is good.

PSALM 106:1 KJV

February 5

*He which hath begun a good work in you
will perform it until the day of Jesus Christ.*

PHILIPPIANS 1:6 KJV

November 26

O give thanks unto the Lord; for He is good.

I CHRONICLES 16:34 KJV

February 6

The beloved of the Lord shall dwell in safety by Him;
and the Lord shall cover him all the day long.

DEUTERONOMY 33:12 KJV

November 25

Enter into His gates with thanksgiving,
and into His courts with praise.

PSALM 100:4 KJV

February 7

Blessed are the poor in spirit:
for theirs is the kingdom of heaven.

MATTHEW 5:3 KJV

November 24

O Lord my God, I will give thanks unto Thee for ever.

PSALM 30:12 KJV

The path of the just is as the shining light,
that shineth more and more unto the perfect day.

PROVERBS 4:18 KJV

November 23

O give thanks unto the Lord; for He is good.

PSALM 136:1 KJV

February 9

Lay up for yourselves treasures in heaven...
For where your treasure is, there will your heart be also.

MATTHEW 6:20, 21 KJV

November 22

Thine, O LORD, is the greatness, and the power, and the glory, and the victory, and the majesty.

I CHRONICLES 29:11 KJV

The Lord shall guide thee continually and satisfy thy soul.

ISAIAH 58:11 KJV

*Rejoice in every good thing
which the Lord thy God hath given unto thee.*

DEUTERONOMY 26:11 KJV

February 11

*Eye hath not seen, nor ear heard...the things which
God hath prepared for them that love Him.*

I CORINTHIANS 2:9 KJV

November 20

*I will cause the shower to come down in his season;
there shall be showers of blessing.*

EZEKIEL 34:26 KJV

Many waters cannot quench love.

SONG OF SOLOMON 8:7 KJV

November 19

O give thanks unto the Lord, for He is good:
for His mercy endureth for ever.

PSALM 107:1 KJV

February 13

We love…because He first loved us.

I JOHN 4:19 KJV

November 18

By Him therefore let us offer the sacrifice of praise to God continually,
that is, the fruit of our lips giving thanks to His name.

HEBREWS 13:15 KJV

February 14

I have loved thee.

ISAIAH 43:4 KJV

November 17

O give thanks unto the Lord; for He is good:
because His mercy endureth for ever.

PSALM 118:1 KJV

February 15

Behold, what manner of love
the Father hath bestowed upon us.

I JOHN 3:1 KJV

November 16

Thanks be to God, which giveth us
the victory through our Lord Jesus Christ.

I CORINTHIANS 15:57 KJV

February 16

His compassions fail not.
They are new every morning: great is Thy faithfulness.

LAMENTATIONS 3:22, 23 KJV

November 15

Unto Thee, O God, do we give thanks.

PSALM 75:1 KJV

February 17

For we are unto God a sweet savour of Christ.

II CORINTHIANS 2:15 KJV

November 14

*My soul doth magnify the Lord,
and my spirit hath rejoiced in God my Saviour.*

LUKE 1:46-47 KJV

February 18

O taste and see that the Lord is good.

PSALM 34:8 KJV

November 13

*And all these blessings shall come on thee, and overtake thee,
if thou shalt hearken unto the voice of the Lord thy God.*

DEUTERONOMY 28:2 KJV

February 19

Jesus Christ the same yesterday, and to day, and for ever.

HEBREWS 13:8 KJV

November 12

Blessed are they which do hunger and thirst after righteousness:
for they shall be filled.

MATTHEW 5:6 KJV

February 20

Thou wilt keep him in perfect peace,
whose mind is stayed on Thee.

ISAIAH 26:3 KJV

November 11

O give thanks unto the Lord; for He is good:
for His mercy endureth for ever.

PSALM 118:29 KJV

Glory and honour are in His presence;
strength and gladness are in His place.

I CHRONICLES 16:27 KJV

November 10

In every thing by prayer and supplication with thanksgiving let your requests be made known unto God.

PHILIPPIANS 4:6 KJV

February 22

The Lord is good to all:
and His tender mercies are over all His works.

PSALM 145:9 KJV

November 9

For the Lord is good; His mercy is everlasting;
and His truth endureth to all generations.

PSALM 100:5 KJV

February 23

The Lord knoweth the days of the upright:
and their inheritance shall be for ever.

PSALM 37:18 KJV

November 8

In every thing give thanks.

I THESSALONIANS 5:18 KJV

February 24

Thou shalt worship the Lord thy God,
and Him only shalt thou serve.

MATTHEW 4:10 KJV

Oh how great is Thy goodness.

PSALM 31:19 KJV

Thy hands have made me and fashioned me.

PSALM 119:73 KJV

November 6

*And whatsoever ye do in word or deed,
do all in the name of the Lord Jesus, giving thanks to God.*

COLOSSIANS 3:17 KJV

February 26

For with God nothing shall be impossible.

LUKE 1:37 KJV

November 5

In Thy presence is fulness of joy;
at Thy right hand there are pleasures for evermore.

PSALM 16:11 KJV

February 27

The Lord shall give that which is good.

PSALM 85:12 KJV

November 4

We give thanks to God and the
Father of our Lord Jesus Christ, praying always for you.

COLOSSIANS 1:3 KJV

February 28

Man shall not live by bread alone,
but by every word that proceedeth out of the mouth of God.

MATTHEW 4:4 KJV

November 3

Stand still, and consider the wondrous works of God.

JOB 37:14 KJV

February 29

*This is the day which the Lord hath made;
we will rejoice and be glad in it.*

PSALM 118:24 KJV

November 2

Giving thanks always for all things unto God.

EPHESIANS 5:20 KJV

March 1

Ye are the light of the world.

MATTHEW 5:14 KJV

November 1

Thy blessing is upon Thy people.

PSALM 3:8 KJV

March 2

The just man walketh in his integrity:
his children are blessed after him.

PROVERBS 20:7 KJV

October 31

Be strong in the Lord, and in the power of His might.

EPHESIANS 6:10 KJV

March 3

God is love; and he that dwelleth in love dwelleth in God, and God in him.

I JOHN 4:16 KJV

I called upon the Lord, and cried to my God:
and He did hear my voice.

II SAMUEL 22:7 KJV

March 4

Let all those that put their trust in Thee rejoice.

PSALM 5:11 KJV

October 29

*The Lord make you to increase
and abound in love one toward another.*

I THESSALONIANS 3:12 KJV

March 5

He that spared not His own Son, but delivered Him up for us all,
how shall He not with Him also freely give us all things?

ROMANS 8:32 KJV

October 28

These words, which I command thee this day, shall be in thine heart: And thou shalt teach them diligently unto thy children.

DEUTERONOMY 6:6-7 KJV

The Lord delighteth in thee.

ISAIAH 62:4 KJV

October 27

Grace, mercy, and peace,
from God our Father and Jesus Christ our Lord.

I TIMOTHY 1:2 KJV

Give, and it shall be given unto you; good measure,
pressed down, and shaken together, and running over.

LUKE 6:38 KJV

October 26

Delight thyself in the Lord;
and I will cause thee to ride upon the high places of the earth.

ISAIAH 58:14 KJV

March 8

How excellent is Thy lovingkindness, O God!

PSALM 36:7 KJV

I am the good shepherd:
the good shepherd giveth His life for the sheep.

JOHN 10:11 KJV

March 9

Truly our fellowship is with the Father,
and with His Son Jesus Christ.

I JOHN 1:3 KJV

October 24

He shall feed His flock like a shepherd: He shall gather the lambs with His arm, and carry them in His bosom.

ISAIAH 40:11 KJV

The blessing of the Lord be upon you.

PSALM 129:8 KJV

October 23

I am the bread of life: he that cometh to Me shall never hunger; and he that believeth on Me shall never thirst.

JOHN 6:35 KJV

March 11

Let us run with patience the race that is set before us.

HEBREWS 12:1 KJV

October 22

Be still, and know that I am God.

PSALM 46:10 KJV

March 12

*O Lord God...with Thy blessing
let the house of Thy servant be blessed for ever.*

II SAMUEL 7:29 KJV

October 21

This is the promise that
He hath promised us, even eternal life.

I JOHN 2:25 KJV

March 13

Thomas Kinkade

Mercy unto you, and peace, and love, be multiplied.

JUDE 1:2 KJV

October 20

Make a joyful noise unto the Lord…
make a loud noise, and rejoice.

PSALM 98:4 KJV

March 14

Serve the Lord with gladness.

PSALM 100:2 KJV

October 19

*The love of God is shed abroad in our hearts
by the Holy Ghost which is given unto us.*

ROMANS 5:5 KJV

*I have no greater joy than to
hear that my children walk in truth.*

III JOHN 1:4 KJV

October 18

Teach me to do Thy will; for Thou art my God:
Thy spirit is good; lead me into the land of uprightness.

PSALM 143:10 KJV

March 16

Make a joyful noise unto the Lord, all ye lands.

PSALM 100:1 KJV

October 17

*Even as the Son of man came not to be ministered unto,
but to minister, and to give His life a ransom for many.*

MATTHEW 20:28 KJV

March 17

The grace of our Lord Jesus Christ be with you.

I CORINTHIANS 16:23 KJV

October 16

The Lord shall bless thee…all the days of thy life.

PSALM 128:5 KJV

March 18

God shall bless thee in all thy works.

DEUTERONOMY 15:10 KJV

October 15

At the name of Jesus every knee should bow, of things in heaven, and things in earth, and things under the earth.

PHILIPPIANS 2:10 KJV

If we walk in the light, as He is in the light,
we have fellowship one with another.

I JOHN 1:7 KJV

October 14

I am the Lord, I change not.

MALACHI 3:6 KJV

March 20

*In all thy ways acknowledge Him,
and He shall direct thy paths.*

PROVERBS 3:6 KJV

October 13

God, who is rich in mercy, for His great love
wherewith He loved us, even when we were dead in sins,
hath quickened us together with Christ, (by grace ye are saved).

EPHESIANS 2:4, 5 KJV

March 21

Blessed be the God…who hath blessed us with all spiritual blessings.

EPHESIANS 1:3 KJV

October 12

Happy is the man that findeth wisdom...Her ways are
ways of pleasantness, and all her paths are peace.

PROVERBS 3:13, 17 KJV

*Know ye that the Lord He is God: it is He that hath made us,
and not we ourselves; we are His people, and the sheep of His pasture.*

PSALM 100:3 KJV

October 11

As Christ was raised up from the dead by the glory of the Father,
even so we also should walk in newness of life.

ROMANS 6:4 KJV

March 23

If we love one another, God dwelleth in us,
and His love is perfected in us.

I JOHN 4:12 KJV

October 10

Thy word is a lamp unto my feet, and a light unto my path.

PSALM 119:105 KJV

March 24

Then shall thy light break forth as the morning,
and thine health shall spring forth speedily.

ISAIAH 58:8 KJV

October 9

Thou only art holy:
for all nations shall come and worship before Thee.

REVELATION 15:4 KJV

March 25

*For it is God which worketh in you
both to will and to do of His good pleasure.*

PHILIPPIANS 2:13 KJV

October 8

They that seek the Lord shall not want any good thing.

PSALM 34:10 KJV

March 26

O sing unto the Lord a new song:
sing unto the Lord, all the earth.

PSALM 96:1 KJV

October 7

My sheep hear My voice, and I know them, and they follow Me.

JOHN 10:27 KJV

God is love; and he that dwelleth in love dwelleth in God.

I JOHN 4:16 KJV

The Lord thy God is with thee whithersoever thou goest.

JOSHUA 1:9 KJV

March 28

To every thing there is a season,
and a time to every purpose under the heaven.

ECCLESIASTES 3:1 KJV

October 5

I am He that liveth, and was dead;
and, behold, I am alive for evermore.

REVELATION 1:18 KJV

March 29

Let your light so shine before men, that they may see your good works, and glorify your Father which is in heaven.

MATTHEW 5:16 KJV

October 4

The Lord thy God, He will go over before thee.

DEUTERONOMY 31:3 KJV

March 30

Our heart shall rejoice in Him.

PSALM 33:21 KJV

October 3

*We see Jesus, who was made a little lower than the angels
for the suffering of death, crowned with glory and honour;
that He by the grace of God should taste death for every man.*

HEBREWS 2:9 KJV

March 31

Love one another, as I have loved you.

JOHN 15:12 KJV

October 2

*I am with thee, and will
keep thee in all places whither thou goest.*

GENESIS 28:15 KJV

April 1

The eternal God is thy refuge,
and underneath are the everlasting arms.

DEUTERONOMY 33:27 KJV

October 1

Behold, the Lion of the tribe of Juda,
the Root of David, hath prevailed.

REVELATION 5:5 KJV

He is not here: for He is risen, as He said.
Come, see the place where the Lord lay.

MATTHEW 28:6 KJV

September 30

Blessed is the man that walketh not in
the counsel of the ungodly…his delight is in the law of the Lord;
and in His law doth he meditate day and night.

PSALM 1:1, 2 KJV

April 3

Therefore my heart is glad, and my glory rejoiceth.

PSALM 16:9 KJV

September 29

As Christ was raised up from the dead by the glory of the Father,
even so we also should walk in newness of life.

ROMANS 6:4 KJV

Go quickly, and tell His disciples
that He is risen from the dead.

MATTHEW 28:7 KJV

September 28

Train up a child in the way he should go:
and when he is old, he will not depart from it.

PROVERBS 22:6 KJV

April 5

O sing unto the Lord a new song;
for He hath done marvellous things.

PSALM 98:1 KJV

September 27

The fruit of the Spirit is love.

GALATIANS 5:22 KJV

Because I live, ye shall live also.

JOHN 14:19 KJV

September 26

He shall be like a tree planted by the rivers of water,
that bringeth forth his fruit in his season.

PSALM 1:3 KJV

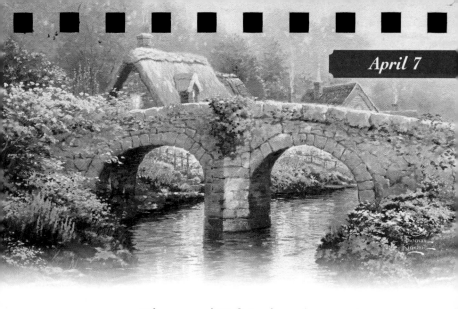

The eternal God is thy refuge.

DEUTERONOMY 33:27 KJV

September 25

If God be for us, who can be against us?

ROMANS 8:31 KJV

April 8

In the world ye shall have tribulation:
but be of good cheer; I have overcome the world.

JOHN 16:33 KJV

September 24

The blessing of the Lord, it maketh rich.

PROVERBS 10:22 KJV

April 9

The Lord is my shepherd.

PSALM 23:1 KJV

September 23

For God sent not His Son into the world to condemn
the world; but that the world through Him might be saved.

JOHN 3:17 KJV

Faith is the substance of things hoped for,
the evidence of things not seen.

HEBREWS 11:1 KJV

September 22

Thou, O Lord, art our Father, our Redeemer;
Thy name is from everlasting.

ISAIAH 63:16 KJV

April 11

Blessed are all they that put their trust in Him.

PSALM 2:12 KJV

September 21

Whatsoever things are lovely...
if there be any praise, think on these things.

PHILIPPIANS 4:8 KJV

April 12

Ye are complete in Him.

COLOSSIANS 2:10 KJV

September 20

My son, keep thy father's commandment,
and forsake not the law of thy mother.

PROVERBS 6:20 KJV

April 13

Trust in the Lord with all thine heart;
and lean not unto thine own understanding.

PROVERBS 3:5 KJV

September 19

Let us offer the sacrifice of praise to God continually,
that is, the fruit of our lips giving thanks to His name.

HEBREWS 13:15 KJV

April 14

*And we know that all things work together
for good to them that love God.*

ROMANS 8:28 KJV

September 18

O magnify the Lord with me, and let us exalt His name together.

PSALM 34:3 KJV

April 15

*He hath put a new song in my mouth,
even praise unto our God.*

PSALM 40:3 KJV

September 17

I am with you always, even unto the end of the world.

MATTHEW 28:20 KJV

April 16

Now unto Him that is able to do exceeding abundantly above all that we ask or think…Unto Him be glory.

EPHESIANS 3:20, 21 KJV

September 16

Though your sins be as scarlet,
they shall be as white as snow.

ISAIAH 1:18 KJV

April 17

Thou hast put gladness in my heart.

PSALM 4:7 KJV

September 15

We love one another.

II JOHN 1:5 KJV

April 18

*Not that we are sufficient of ourselves to think
any thing as of ourselves; but our sufficiency is of God.*

II CORINTHIANS 3:5 KJV

September 14

The Spirit of the Lord God is upon me…to give unto them beauty for ashes, the oil of joy for mourning, the garment of praise for the spirit of heaviness.

ISAIAH 61:1, 3 KJV

April 19

I the Lord…will hold thine hand, and will keep thee.

ISAIAH 42:6 KJV

September 13

I am come a light into the world, that whosoever
believeth on Me should not abide in darkness.

JOHN 12:46 KJV

April 20

Rejoice with them that do rejoice.

ROMANS 12:15 KJV

September 12

*Arise, shine; for thy light is come,
and the glory of the Lord is risen upon thee.*

ISAIAH 60:1 KJV

Commit thy way unto the LORD;
trust also in Him; and He shall bring it to pass.

PSALM 37:5 KJV

September 11

Let us draw near with a true heart in full assurance of faith.

HEBREWS 10:22 KJV

April 22

Of His fulness have all we received, and grace for grace.

JOHN 1:16 KJV

September 10

For Thou art great,
and doest wondrous things: Thou art God alone.

PSALM 86:10 KJV

April 23

Let the beauty of the Lord our God be upon us.

PSALM 90:17 KJV

September 9

But we all, with open face beholding as in a glass the glory of the Lord, are changed into the same image from glory to glory, even as by the Spirit of the Lord.

II CORINTHIANS 3:18 KJV

April 24

And now abideth faith, hope, charity, these three;
but the greatest of these is charity.

I CORINTHIANS 13:13 KJV

September 8

My voice shalt Thou hear in the morning, O Lord;
in the morning will I direct my prayer unto Thee, and will look up.

PSALM 5:3 KJV

April 25

Seek the Lord and His strength, seek His face continually.

I CHRONICLES 16:11 KJV

September 7

I commend you to God, and to the word of His grace,
which is able to build you up.

ACTS 20:32 KJV

April 26

God is not unrighteous to forget your work and labour of love, which ye have shewed toward His name.

HEBREWS 6:10 KJV

September 6

I have put My words in thy mouth, and I have covered thee in the shadow of Mine hand…thou art My people.

ISAIAH 51:16 KJV

April 27

Marvellous are Thy works.

PSALM 139:14 KJV

September 5

My yoke is easy, and My burden is light.

MATTHEW 11:30 KJV

April 28

*Be ye stedfast, unmovable, always abounding in the work of the Lord,
forasmuch as ye know that your labour is not in vain in the Lord.*

I CORINTHIANS 15:58 KJV

September 4

The LORD will command his lovingkindness in the daytime, and in the night His song shall be with me, and my prayer unto the God of my life.

PSALM 42:8 KJV

April 29

As for God, His way is perfect.

PSALM 18:30 KJV

September 3

Take My yoke upon you, and learn of Me; for I am meek and lowly in heart: and ye shall find rest unto your souls.

MATTHEW 11:29 KJV

April 30

The fruit of the Spirit is in all goodness.

EPHESIANS 5:9 KJV

September 2

The Lord that made heaven and earth bless thee.

PSALM 134:3 KJV

May 1

Wait on the Lord...and He shall strengthen thine heart.

PSALM 27:14 KJV

September 1

We have seen and do testify that the Father
sent the Son to be the Saviour of the world.

I JOHN 4:14 KJV

Draw nigh to God, and He will draw nigh to you.

JAMES 4:8 KJV

August 31

Behold, God is my salvation; I will trust, and not be afraid: for the Lord Jehovah is my strength and my song; He also is become my salvation.

ISAIAH 12:2 KJV

May 3

The LORD is a great God, and a great King above all gods.

PSALM 95:3 KJV

August 30

Remembering without ceasing your work of faith,
and labour of love, and patience of hope in our Lord Jesus Christ.

I THESSALONIANS 1:2, 3 KJV

May 4

Blessed be God, even the Father of our Lord Jesus Christ, the Father of mercies, and the God of all comfort.

II CORINTHIANS 1:3 KJV

August 29

The Lord hath been mindful of us: He will bless us.

PSALM 115:12 KJV

May 5

The ransomed of the Lord shall return,
and come to Zion with songs and everlasting joy.

ISAIAH 35:10 KJV

August 28

*Being found in fashion as a man, He humbled himself,
and became obedient unto death, even the death of the cross.*

PHILIPPIANS 2:8 KJV

I will not leave you comfortless: I will come to you.

JOHN 14:18 KJV

August 27

The Lord preserveth all them that love Him.

PSALM 145:20 KJV

May 7

Happy is he…whose hope is in the Lord his God.

PSALM 146:5 KJV

August 26

For all have sinned, and come short of the glory of God.

ROMANS 3:23 KJV

May 8

Now we see through a glass, darkly; but then face to face.

I CORINTHIANS 13:12 KJV

August 25

The Lord be with you.

RUTH 2:4 KJV

I am the Lord that healeth thee.

EXODUS 15:26 KJV

August 24

The gift of God is eternal life through Jesus Christ our Lord.

ROMANS 6:23 KJV

May 10

I go and prepare a place for you, I will come again, and receive you unto Myself; that where I am, there ye may be also.

JOHN 14:3 KJV

August 23

The Lord is my rock, and my fortress...
my strength, in whom I will trust.

PSALM 18:2 KJV

May 11

The goodness of God endureth continually.

PSALM 52:1 KJV

August 22

In the beginning was the Word,
and the Word was with God, and the Word was God.

JOHN 1:1 KJV

May 12

I am the resurrection, and the life:
he that believeth in Me…shall never die.

JOHN 11:25, 26 KJV

August 21

Blessed is the people that know the joyful sound:
they shall walk, O Lord, in the light of Thy countenance.

PSALM 89:15 KJV

My help cometh from the Lord,
which made heaven and earth.

PSALM 121:2 KJV

This is life eternal, that they might know Thee the only true God.

JOHN 17:3 KJV

May 14

Bear ye one another's burdens.

GALATIANS 6:2 KJV

August 19

Send out Thy light and Thy truth: let them lead me.

PSALM 43:3 KJV

May 15

Let, I pray Thee, Thy merciful kindness be for my comfort.

PSALM 119:76 KJV

August 18

In Him was life; and the life was the light of men.

JOHN 1:4 KJV

*Come unto Me, all ye that...are heavy laden,
and I will give you rest.*

MATTHEW 11:28 KJV

August 17

Give unto the Lord the glory due unto His name.

PSALM 96:8 KJV

May 17

With His stripes we are healed.

ISAIAH 53:5 KJV

August 16

For He that is mighty hath done to me great things;
and holy is His name.

LUKE 1:49 KJV

May 18

Grace be with you, mercy, and peace, from God the Father,
and from the Lord Jesus Christ.

II JOHN 1:3 KJV

August 15

Give unto the Lord glory and strength.

PSALM 96:7 KJV

May 19

Thou art with me; Thy rod and Thy staff they comfort me.

PSALM 23:4 KJV

August 14

Blessed are the peacemakers:
for they shall be called the children of God.

MATTHEW 5:9 KJV

May 20

*My God shall supply all your need
according to His riches in glory by Christ Jesus.*

PHILIPPIANS 4:19 KJV

August 13

From the end of the earth will I cry unto Thee...
lead me to the rock that is higher than I.

PSALM 61:2 KJV

May 21

With Thee is the fountain of life: in Thy light shall we see light.

PSALM 36:9 KJV

August 12

Blessed are the pure in heart: for they shall see God.

MATTHEW 5:8 KJV

May 22

*We are confident, I say, and willing rather
to be absent from the body, and to be present with the Lord.*

II CORINTHIANS 5:8 KJV

August 11

*The earth shall be full of the knowledge of the Lord,
as the waters cover the sea.*

ISAIAH 11:9 KJV

May 23

*Call unto Me, and I will answer thee,
and shew thee great and mighty things, which thou knowest not.*

JEREMIAH 33:3 KJV

August 10

Blessed are the merciful: for they shall obtain mercy.

MATTHEW 5:7 KJV

May 24

Whatsoever ye do, do it heartily,
as to the Lord, and not unto men.

COLOSSIANS 3:23 KJV

*In God is my salvation and my glory:
the rock of my strength, and my refuge, is in God.*

PSALM 62:7 KJV

May 25

For He shall give His angels charge over thee,
to keep thee in all thy ways.

PSALM 91:11 KJV

August 8

For the hope which is laid up for you in heaven,
whereof ye heard before in the word of the truth of the gospel.

COLOSSIANS 1:5 KJV

May 26

Of the Lord ye shall receive the reward of the inheritance:
for ye serve the Lord Christ.

COLOSSIANS 3:24 KJV

August 7

Behold, I will do a new thing; now it shall spring forth.

ISAIAH 43:19 KJV

May 27

The eyes of the Lord are upon the righteous,
and His ears are open unto their cry.

PSALM 34:15 KJV

August 6

In every thing ye are enriched by Him,
in all utterance, and in all knowledge.

I CORINTHIANS 1:5 KJV

May 28

If two of you shall agree on earth as touching any thing that they shall ask, it shall be done for them of My Father which is in heaven.

MATTHEW 18:19 KJV

August 5

It is good that a man should both
hope and quietly wait for the salvation of the Lord.

LAMENTATIONS 3:26 KJV

May 29

My presence shall go with thee, and I will give thee rest.

EXODUS 33:14 KJV

August 4

God is love.

I JOHN 4:8 KJV

May 30

One Lord, one faith, one baptism.

EPHESIANS 4:5 KJV

August 3

Praise the Lord, call upon His name, declare His doings among the people, make mention that His name is exalted.

ISAIAH 12:4 KJV

May 31

As the mountains are round about Jerusalem,
so the Lord is round about His people.

PSALM 125:2 KJV

August 2

*For whom He did foreknow, He also did predestinate
to be conformed to the image of His Son.*

ROMANS 8:29 KJV

June 1

As many of you as have been
baptized into Christ have put on Christ.

GALATIANS 3:27 KJV

August 1

Make a joyful noise before the Lord, the King.

PSALM 98:6 KJV

June 2

Our soul waiteth for the Lord: He is our help and our shield.

PSALM 33:20 KJV

July 31

Sin shall not have dominion over you:
for ye are not under the law, but under grace.

ROMANS 6:14 KJV

June 3

With God all things are possible.

MATTHEW 19:26 KJV

July 30

In the house of the righteous is much treasure.

PROVERBS 15:6 KJV

June 4

For Thou art my hope, O Lord God: Thou art my trust.

PSALM 71:5 KJV

July 29

The God of our Lord Jesus Christ, the Father of glory, may give unto you the spirit of wisdom and revelation in the knowledge of Him.

EPHESIANS 1:17 KJV

June 5

Present your bodies a living sacrifice,
holy, acceptable unto God.

ROMANS 12:1 KJV

July 28

This book of the law shall not depart out of thy mouth;
but thou shalt meditate therein day and night.

JOSHUA 1:8 KJV

June 6

I will greatly rejoice in the Lord...
for He hath clothed me with the garments of salvation.

ISAIAH 61:10 KJV

July 27

Who shall separate us from the love of Christ?

ROMANS 8:35 KJV

June 7

Jesus Christ himself…
stablish you in every good word and work.

II THESSALONIANS 2:16, 17 KJV

July 26

My Spirit that is upon thee, and My words which
I have put in thy mouth, shall not depart out of thy mouth.

ISAIAH 59:21 KJV

June 8

Blessed be the LORD God, the God of Israel,
who only doeth wondrous things.

PSALMS 72:18 KJV

July 25

Thou art worthy, O Lord,
to receive glory and honour and power.

REVELATION 4:11 KJV

June 9

*The fruit of righteousness is
sown in peace of them that make peace.*

JAMES 3:18 KJV

July 24

The Lord hath comforted His people, and will have mercy.

ISAIAH 49:13 KJV

June 10

God is our refuge and strength, a very present help.

PSALM 46:1 KJV

July 23

We have peace with God through our Lord Jesus Christ.

ROMANS 5:1 KJV

June 11

*For this cause I bow my knees
unto the Father of our Lord Jesus Christ.*

EPHESIANS 3:14 KJV

July 22

*I will instruct thee and teach thee
in the way which thou shalt go.*

PSALM 32:8 KJV

June 12

I have loved thee with an everlasting love.

JEREMIAH 31:3 KJV

July 21

By love serve one another.

GALATIANS 5:13 KJV

June 13

I can do all things through Christ which strengtheneth me.

PHILIPPIANS 4:13 KJV

July 20

*Make me to go in the path of Thy commandments;
for therein do I delight.*

PSALM 119:35 KJV

June 14

He is my refuge and my fortress:
my God; in Him will I trust.

PSALM 91:2 KJV

July 19

I have you in my heart.

PHILIPPIANS 1:7 KJV

June 15

Be kindly affectioned one to another...
in honour preferring one another.

ROMANS 12:10 KJV

July 18

One generation shall praise Thy works to another, and shall declare Thy mighty acts.

PSALM 145:4 KJV

June 16

The Lord is good unto them that wait for Him.

LAMENTATIONS 3:25 KJV

July 17

Rooted and built up in Him, and stablished in the faith...
abounding therein with thanksgiving.

COLOSSIANS 2:7 KJV

June 17

Greater is He that is in you, than he that is in the world.

I JOHN 4:4 KJV

July 16

I am thy God: I will strengthen thee; yea, I will help thee.

ISAIAH 41:10 KJV

June 18

Great is the Lord, and greatly to be praised.

PSALM 145:3 KJV

July 15

For we are His workmanship, created in Christ Jesus unto good works,
which God hath before ordained that we should walk in them.

EPHESIANS 2:10 KJV

June 19

*Therefore if any man be in Christ, he is a new creature:
old things are passed away; behold, all things are become new.*

II CORINTHIANS 5:17 KJV

July 14

The Lord hath done great things for us; whereof we are glad.

PSALM 126:3 KJV

June 20

Delight thyself also in the Lord;
and He shall give thee the desires of thine heart.

PSALM 37:4 KJV

July 13

Love one another with a pure heart fervently.

I PETER 1:22 KJV

June 21

For God so loved the world,
that He gave His only begotten Son.

JOHN 3:16 KJV

July 12

"For I know the thoughts that I think toward you," saith the Lord, "thoughts of peace, and not of evil, to give you an expected end."

JEREMIAH 29:11 KJV

June 22

Know that the LORD hath set apart him that is godly for Himself:
the LORD will hear when I call unto Him.

PSALM 4:3 KJV

July 11

Charity never faileth.

I CORINTHIANS 13:8 KJV

June 23

This is the confidence that we have in Him, that,
if we ask any thing according to His will, He heareth us.

I JOHN 5:14 KJV

July 10

The Lord will perfect that which concerneth me:
Thy mercy, O Lord, endureth for ever.

PSALM 138:8 KJV

June 24

The Lord thy God in the midst of thee is mighty;
He will save, He will rejoice over thee with joy;
He will rest in His love, He will joy over thee with singing.

ZEPHANIAH 3:17 KJV

July 9

*Know the love of Christ, which passeth knowledge,
that ye might be filled with all the fulness of God.*

EPHESIANS 3:19 KJV

June 25

Let us hold fast the profession of our faith without wavering;
For He is faithful that promised.

HEBREWS 10:23 KJV

July 8

He will love thee, and bless thee.

DEUTERONOMY 7:13 KJV

June 26

*The Lord shall preserve thy going out and thy coming in
from this time forth, and even for evermore.*

PSALM 121:8 KJV

July 7

We are more than conquerors through Him that loved us.

ROMANS 8:37 KJV

June 27

These things have I spoken unto you, that My joy might remain in you, and that your joy might be full.

JOHN 15:11 KJV

July 6

Children are an heritage of the Lord:
and the fruit of the womb is His reward.

PSALM 127:3 KJV

Ye are blessed of the Lord which made heaven and earth.

PSALM 115:15 KJV

July 5

Beloved, let us love one another: for love is of God.

I JOHN 4:7 KJV

June 29

Edify one another, even as also ye do.

I THESSALONIANS 5:11 KJV

July 4

Every word of God is pure:
He is a shield unto them that put their trust in Him.

PROVERBS 30:5 KJV

June 30

I carry you: I have made, and I will bear;
even I will carry, and will deliver you.

ISAIAH 46:4 KJV

July 3

For we have not an high priest which
cannot be touched with the feeling of our infirmities.

HEBREWS 4:15 KJV

July 1

And all things, whatsoever ye shall
ask in prayer, believing, ye shall receive.

MATTHEW 21:22 KJV

July 2

The Lord is thy keeper:
the Lord is thy shade upon thy right hand.

PSALM 121:5 KJV